Author Tommy Kimball

Illustrator Tiffany Rives

Who

Taught the

Animals?

?

?

?

?

WestBow Press books may be ordered through booksellers or by contacting:

WestBow Press
A Division of Thomas Nelson & Zondervan
1663 Liberty Drive
Bloomington, IN 47403
www.westbowpress.com
844-714-3454

Interior Image Credit: Tiffany Rives

KJV: Scripture taken from the King James Version of the Bible.

ISBN: 978-1-6642-7942-1 (sc)
ISBN: 978-1-6642-7944-5 (hc)
ISBN: 978-1-6642-7943-8 (e)

Library of Congress Control Number: 2022917970

Print information available on the last page.

WestBow Press rev. date: 10/10/2022

WestBow
PRESS®
A DIVISION OF THOMAS NELSON
& ZONDERVAN

Dedication

This book is dedicated to my late wife, Betty Kimball. She was a committed Christian woman. I began my ministry over 60 years ago now with her at my side. I could not have been more blessed. She was the perfect preacher's wife. She was a loving mother, grandmother, and great-grandmother. She looked at God's creation with such wonder and appreciation. One of her most favorites of God's creation was the redbird. I can only imagine what she is seeing now in the presence of our Lord!

Acknowledgements

I would like to thank Tiffany Rives for the beautiful illustrations that reflect the uniqueness of each of these animals that God created and for framing them in such an engaging manner. I would like to thank my daughter, Kay Rodriguez, who included some of my poems in the book she published, "The Visits" and was inspired by prayer to encourage me to turn one of my poems into a children's book. I would like to thank my son-in-law, Joe Rodriguez, whose business acumen and wisdom have always been available for me to lean on. Finally, I would like to thank the elders of my church who helped sponsor the development of this book that not only acknowledges God's creation, but also shares the most important message of all; the message of salvation that comes through the birth, death, and resurrection of His son, Jesus Christ!

Who taught the birds to
fly from tree to tree?

Who taught the fish to swim
in the deep of the sea?

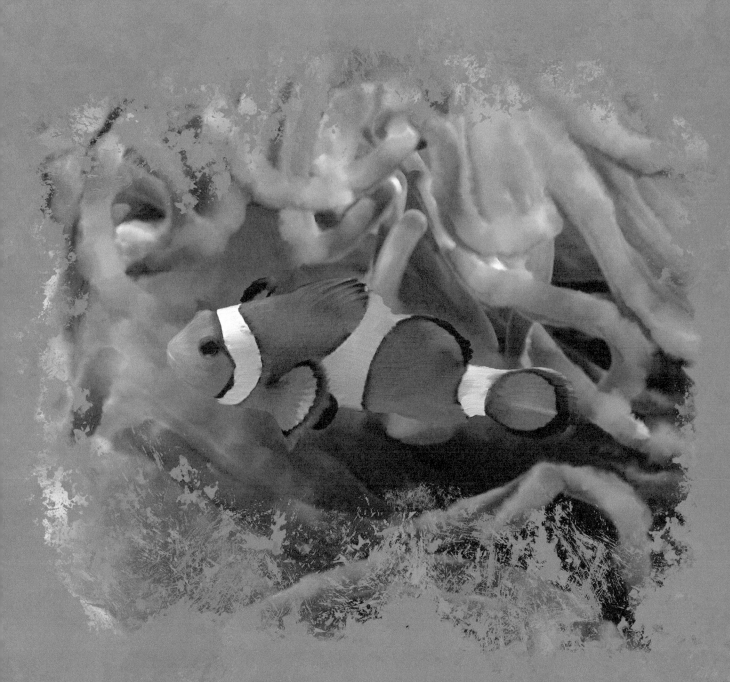

Who taught the kangaroo to jump in the land down under?

Who taught the horse about his strength and clothes his neck with thunder? Reference Job 39:19

Who taught the eagle to screech from so high up in the sky?

Who taught the lion to roar and in his cunning be so sly?

Who taught the cheetah to run faster than all the rest?

Who taught the owl to hoot
deep in the night in his nest?

17

Who taught the turkey to gobble and spread his tail feathers like a fan?

Who taught the dog to bark and be the best friend to man?

Who taught the cat to meow and purr so sweetly?

Who taught the lamb to baa and follow the shepherd so meekly?

25

Only God, creator of all,
instilled it in all of them.

27

And when time is no more,

they will give their praise to Him.

29

And every creature which is in Heaven, and on the Earth, and under the Earth, and such as are in the sea, and all that are in them, heard I saying, Blessing, and honor, and glory, and power, be unto him that sitteth upon the throne, and unto the Lamb for ever and ever.

Revelation 5:13 KJV

Holy Bible

In the beginning God created

the heaven and earth... *Genesis 1:1 KJV*

That if thou shalt confess with thy mouth the Lord Jesus, and shalt believe in thine heart that God hath raised him from the dead, thou shalt be saved.

Romans 10:9 KJV

For with the heart man believeth unto righteousness; and with the mouth confession is made unto salvation.

Romans 10:10 KJV

Printed in the United States
by Baker & Taylor Publisher Services